for violin
Book 2 (silver)

£8.95

Georgia Vale

in the book:

- pieces using up to 4 fingers, and low 2nd finger
- slurs and double stopping
- introduction to G, D, A and E majors
- longer 'concert' pieces - some in two-parts, like a duet!
- note charts, quizzes and 'be a composer' sections
- 'what it all means' page
- certificate

on the CD:

- The top number indicates the complete performance, and the bottom number the accompaniment alone.

- When there is no introduction in the accompaniment, beats will be given for 2 full bars, or 1 full bar and part of a bar.

- Track 1 is a tuning track.

© Copyright Georgia Vale 2009
All rights reserved

Published by Hey Presto Strings, Bromsgrove, Worcs
www.heyprestostrings.com

Printed and bound in England by Pace Print & Design, Worcester
Design of the characters Presto, Bravo and Poco, by Nathalie Walters

Contents

	Page
3 fingers - reading the music	1
1. Cradle song	2
2. Halloween haunt	2
3. Sunny days	3
4. Under the sea	3
5. Song for Eleanor	4
6. I'm not too sure	4
Quavers	5
7. Headlong	6
8. Cherry singers	6
9. The lonely stars	7
10. Woodpecker	7
11. This old man	8
12. By the old willow tree	8
Slurs	9
13. The river	10
14. Sleeping under the stars	10
15. Then and there	11
16. Knickerbocker glory	11
17. Under the weather	12
18. Lonely moon	12
The 4th finger	13
19. Mary had a little lamb	14
20. Danger, danger	14
21. Suit yourself	15
22. Train whistle	15
23. A la Bach!	16
24. Over the moon	16
25. Cuban blues	17
Dotted crotchets	18
26. Ode to joy	19
27. Jingle bells	19
28. Chimes	19
29. Scotch mist	20
30. Travellin' home	21
31. Just a little tube of toothpaste	21
32. Monsoon	22
33. The Grand Canyon	22

	Page
Low 2nd fingers	23
The key of G major	24
34. Rosie's waltz	25
35. Boa constrictor	25
36. Get a move on	26
37. Early days	27
38. Peachy	27
D, A & E majors	28
39. Come sway with me	29
40. Risky business	29
41. Calypso	30
42. Allegro in E	30
Concert pieces	
43. Old song	31
44. Andantino (violin 1)	32
Andantino (violin 2)	33
45. Sleepyhead (violin 1)	34
Sleepyhead (violin 2)	35
46. Fiddle fiesta (violin 1)	36
Fiddle fiesta (violin 2)	37
Some rhythms to try!	38
Presto's quiz	39
What it all means!	40
Certificate	41

3 fingers - reading the music

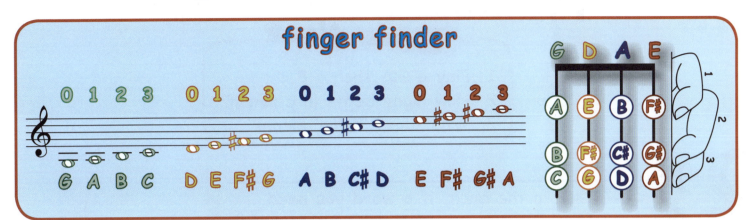

Odd number fingers are line notes, even number fingers are space notes!

Exercise 1

Exercise 2

Exercise 3

Exercise 4

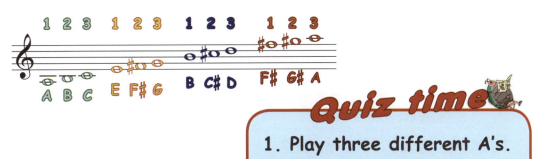

Quiz time

1. Play three different A's.
2. Point to a tied note.
3. What does *mp* mean?

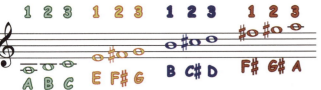

Quiz time

1. What does 'rit.' mean?
2. How many beats in each bar?
3. Point to an up bow D.

Are your fingers really right?
Or are they holding on too tight?

5. Song for Eleanor

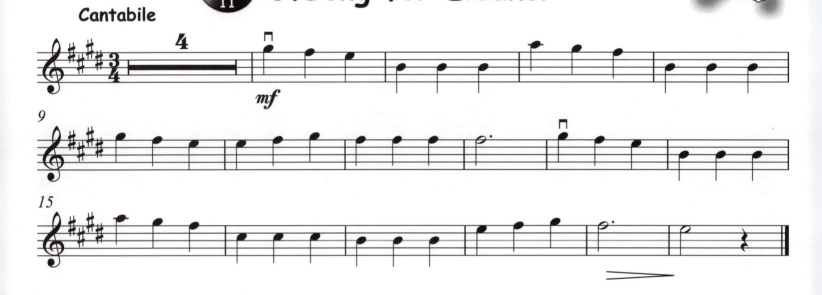

Cantabile

6. I'm not too sure

Cantabile

mf I'm not too sure, not a - ny more. How will I e - ver turn

o - ver? *f* I've tried so hard, my shell is scarred!

Help me, please help me turn o - ver!

Quavers

 The Quaver twins like to go quite fast, and when they're together they often join up their tails:

I think this means one of the twins is taking a rest.

quaver ½ beat

Play rhythms!

 Make rhythms using quavers and other time values!

If you're not sure of the beat, you'll find those words are pretty neat!

thick, goo-ey lem-on curd

tick-y tock-y tick tock

please don't tick-le me

Be a composer!
Use the rhythms you know to make up a tune!

Title ....

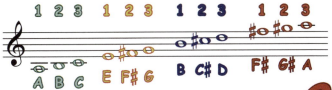

Quiz time

1. What does 'allegro' mean?
2. Play a C♯, then an F♯.
3. Point to a repeat mark.

9. The lonely stars

Distantly

mp We're so lone - ly, ve - ry lone - ly, why must we all be so far a - part? How can we make friends with each - o - ther, warm our cold and lone - ly hearts?

Those > signs are accents. Make the accented notes stronger - like the woodpecker tapping.

10. Woodpecker

Allegro

mf

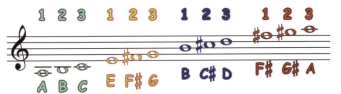

Quiz time

1. What does *mf* mean?
2. Play two different G's.
3. What does 'andante' mean?

Andante

11. This old man

Traditional

Do you like the sound you hear?
Is it tuneful, nice and clear?

12. By the old willow tree

Espressivo

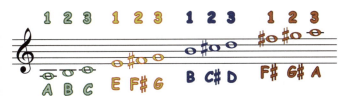

Slurs

A slur joins *different* notes, to make a smooth sound. Play all the notes in a slur with *one* bow!

Slurs make music nice and smooth, they make it ebb and flow.
So change your fingers in each slur, but do not change the bow!

Exercise 1

Exercise 2

Exercise 3

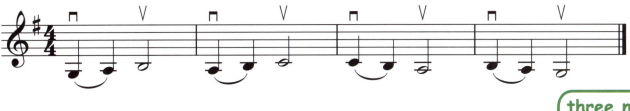

Exercise 4

three notes to one bow...!

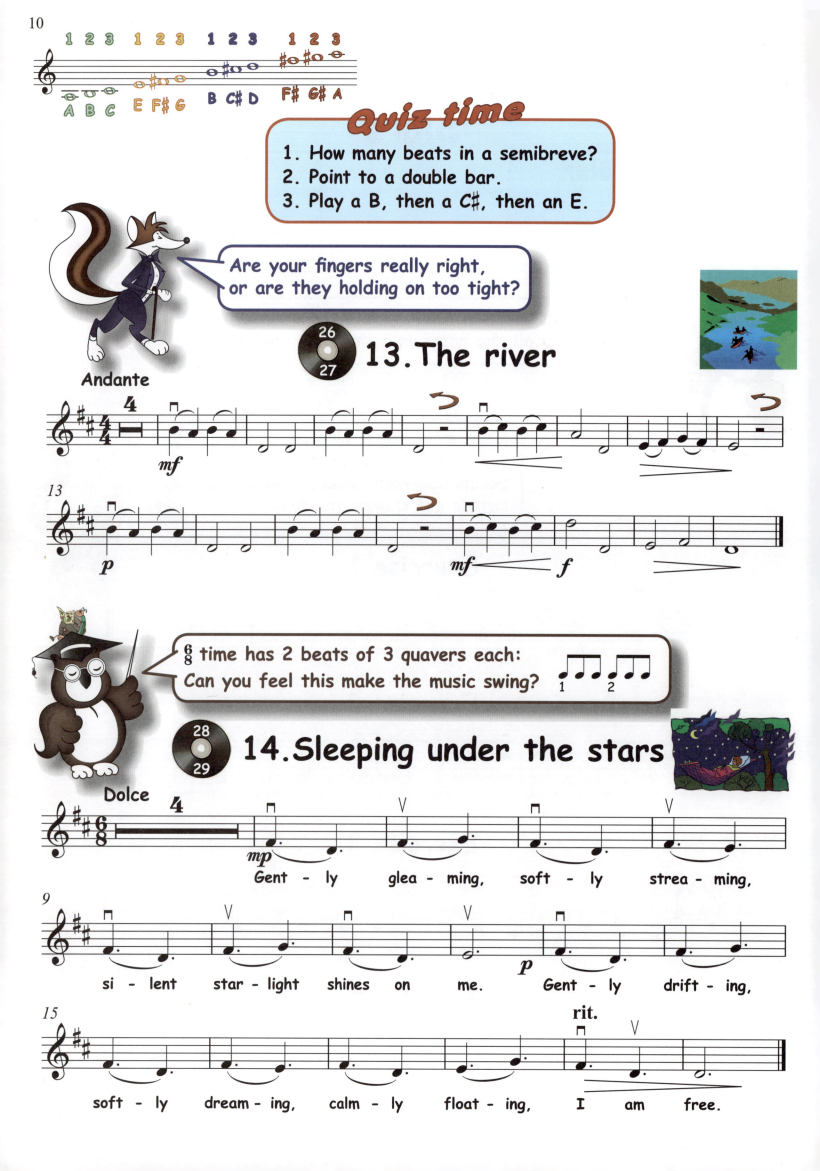

Quiz time

1. What does 'energico' mean?
2. How many beats in each bar?
3. Name the notes on the A string.

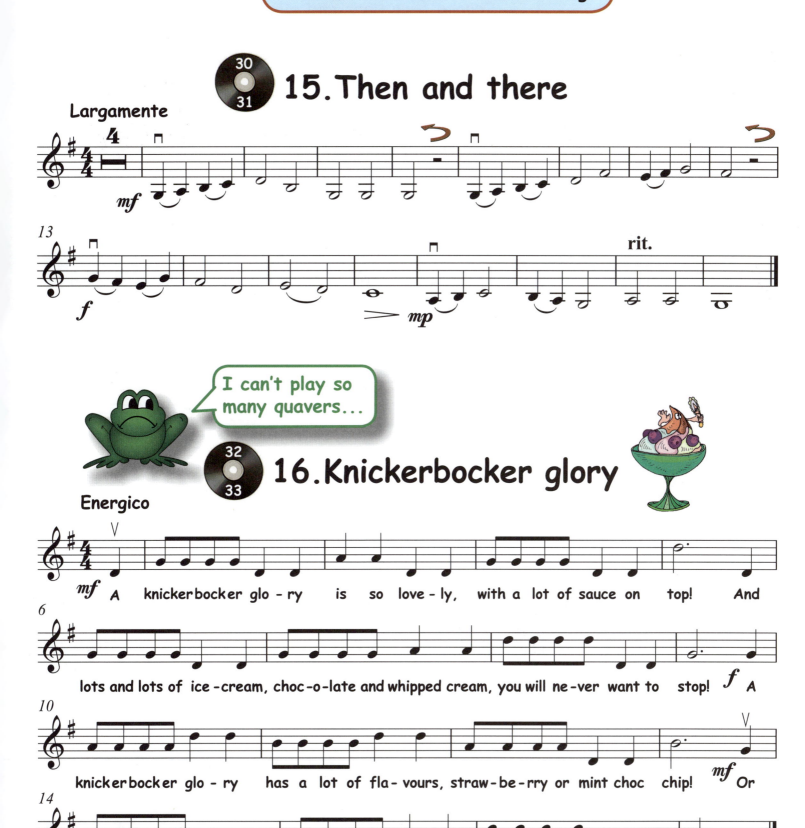

The 4th finger

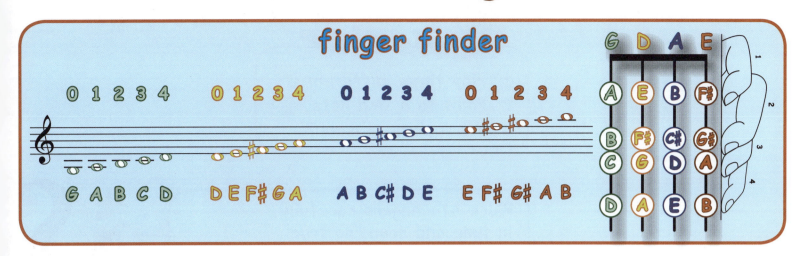

The 4th finger makes the same note as the next string up!

Open string notes D, A and E, these you've learned to play. 4th finger now will find all three, and play them a new way!

Exercise 1

Exercise 2

Exercise 3

Exercise 4

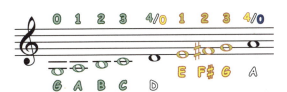

Quiz time

1. Choose four different notes, and name them!
2. What note does 4th finger make on the G string?
3. Point to a harmonic sign.

 21. Suit yourself

 I blew into the f-hole by accident, and it made a train sound!

 22. Train whistle

Quiz time

1. Point to a 1st-time bar.
2. Play a harmonic on the A string.
3. How many beats in a quaver?

Johann Sebastian Bach was a German composer who lived from 1685 to 1750. This music is written in his style!

23. A la Bach!

24. Over the moon

Quiz time

1. Clap the 1st four bars.
2. What does 'moderato' mean?
3. Point to a 'staccato' sign.

Presto said I missed a beat, said my notes were incomplete! Said it's Poco's sound that's sweet, and Poco's slurs that are so neat!

Ohh...!

25. Cuban blues

Dotted crotchets

Dotted crotchet waits for 1½ beats before she moves.

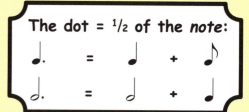

The dot = ½ of the *note*:

dotted crotchet
1½ beats

Here's Dotty crotchet's rest:

Play rhythms!

You know what to do!

Try these rhythms now with me –
I'm sure you'll find them trouble-free!

dream   of cakes and cream...

spoo-ky hal-low-een   to-night

bum - ble bee, bum - ble bee

Be a composer!
Use the rhythms you know to make up a tune!

Title ....

Quiz time

1. Point to an F♯, a G, and a C♯.
2. How many beats in a dotted crotchet?
3. Find a slur and a tie!

26. Ode to joy
L. van Beethoven

27. Jingle bells
J Pierpont

28. Chimes

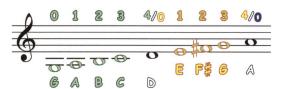
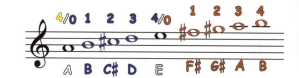

Quiz time

1. Clap the last line.
2. What does 'sempre cresc.' mean?
3. Play two different D's.

Help! Too long! I can't do it!

29. Scotch mist

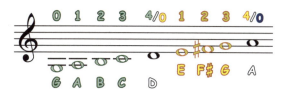

Quiz time

1. Choose eight bars, and clap them!
2. What does 'D.S. al fine' mean?
3. How many beats in a dotted crotchet?

30. Travellin' home

31. Just a little tube of toothpaste

Green - G string
Yellow - D string
Blue - A string
Red - E string

Low 2nd fingers

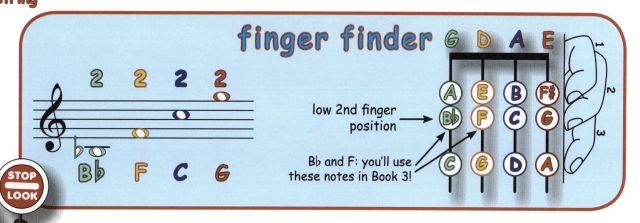

Low 2nd fingers can make music sound sad - a *minor* sound!

High 2nd fingers can make a happy sound - major!

Major makes a happy sound,
and minor makes a sad sound.
It's not so hard so don't you frown,
just move your 2nd up or down!

Can You?

Play these exercises with a high 2nd finger (close to the 3rd finger),
then with a low 2nd finger

Exercise 1

0 1 2 — | 2 1 0 — | 1 2 3 3 | 2 1 0 — ||

Exercise 2

0 0 2 0 | 1 2 3 — | 0 0 3 1 | 2 1 0 — ||

Exercise 3

0 1 2 3 | 0 — 2 — | 0 1 2 1 | 0 — — — ||

Exercise 4

0 0 2 0 | 3 2 1 1 | 1 0 3 0 | 2 1 0 — ||

The key of G major

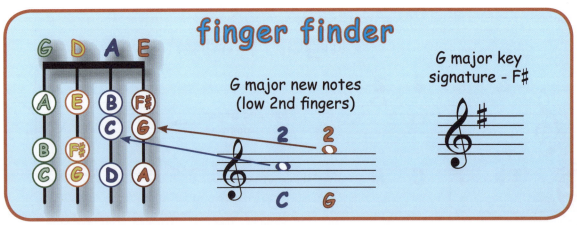

Quiz time

1. What notes can you make with low 2nd fingers?
2. Clap all of 'Boa constrictor'!
3. What does 'pizz.' mean?

Now the notes you ought to know, and by this point they should just flow. So at the top, from now, will show only 2nd fingers low!

34. Rosie's waltz

35. Boa constrictor

Quiz time
1. Point to a 'crescendo' sign.
2. What does *ff* stand for?
3. Play two different G's.

37. Early days

38. Peachy

D, A and E majors

Later, you'll learn more new finger positions for D, A and E majors - but *just for now*:

G major	D major	A & E majors
low 2nds on A and E strings	low 2nd on E string	no low 2nd fingers!

...how can I play A major scale and arpeggio?!

If D major you can play,
A major too will be ok.
Do not change a single thing -
just start it on the A string!

D major scale
(play with and without slurs)

D major arpeggio

Quiz time

1. Clap the first line of 'Risky business'.
2. Point to a low 2nd finger note.
3. What key is 'Come sway with me in'?

39. Come sway with me

40. Risky business

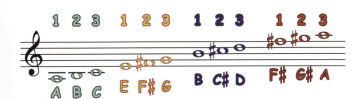

Concert piece 2

Concert piece 3

Play me, sing me, then you'll know when to pluck and when to bow!

45. Sleepyhead
Violin two - 3 fingers and low 2nd

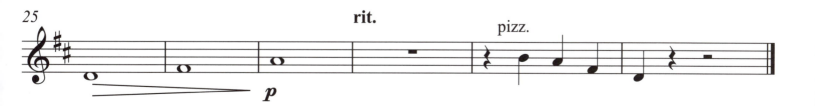

Some rhythms to try!

Lots of rhythms here to try,
lots of them to mystify!
Clap them loudly, make a din,
or play them on your violin!

Presto's quiz

"I might get some right…"

15/20 or more: Fantastic!
10/20 or more: Well done!
5/20 or more: Not too bad…
Less than 5/20: Oh dear…

"Test yourself with my quiz!"

1. Which of these means 'very loud'?

   mp   f   mf   ff

2. Name this note:

   ....

3. What does 'dolce' mean?

   ....

4. Draw a dotted crotchet: ☐

5. How many quavers in a minim?

   6   3   2   4

6. Is this a slur or a tie?

   slur   tie

7. What does 'crescendo' mean?

   ....

8. What is this sign called?

   accent   harmonic   staccato

9. How many crotchets in a semibreve?

   4   1   5   2

10. What note does low 2nd finger make on the A string?

    D   C♯   F   C

11. What does 'con moto' mean?

    ....

12. How many beats in a dotted crotchet?

    1½   2   3   ½

13. What does 'presto' mean?

    ....

14. Should you squeeze your thumb?

    yes   no

15. Circle the 4th finger note:

    F   D   G   C

16. True or false?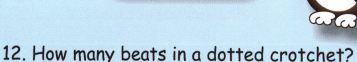

    true   false

17. How many beats in a quaver?

    2   ½   3   ¼

18. Draw a C♯: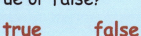

19. What does this sign mean?

    ....

20. What note does 3rd finger make on the G string?

    F♯   B   G   C

What it all means!

Italian words

al fine	to the end
allegro	fast and lively
agitato	agitated
allegretto	lively (but less than allegro)
andante	at a walking speed
arco	use the bow
bravo	well done!
cantabile	in a singing style
con brio	vigorously
con moto	with movement
cresc.	(crescendo) get louder
dim.	(diminuendo) get quieter
dolce	sweetly
Da capo (D.C.)	from the start
D.S.	from the sign 𝄋
energico	with energy
espressivo	expressively
fine	the end
giocoso	merrily
grandioso	grandly
largamente	broadly
leggiero	lightly
misterioso	misteriously
moderato	at a moderate speed
pizz.	(pizzicato) pluck
poco	little
presto	very fast
risoluto	boldly
rit.	(ritardando) slow down
ritmico	rhythmically
semplice	simply
sempre	always
sonore	sonorous, full-toned

New time values

♩.	dotted crotchet - 1½ beats
𝄽.	dotted crotchet rest - 1½ beats
♪	quaver - ½ beat
𝄾	quaver rest - ½ beat

Dynamics

f	loud
mf	moderately (quite) loud
ff	very loud
p	soft, quiet
mp	moderately (quite) quiet
pp	very quiet
&lt;	crescendo - get louder
&gt;	diminuendo - get quieter

Everything else!

2/4	time signature - 2 beats in every bar
:‖ ‖:	repeat marks
♯	a sharp
♭	a flat
♩‿♩	tie - joins 2 or more of the *same* note, making 1 long note
♩‿♩	slur - 2 or more *different* notes in the same bow
♩°	harmonic - a sound effect
♩+	pluck with the left hand
♩. ♩.	staccato dots - play short
♩− ♩−	tenuto marks - not so short!
♩>	accent - play strongly
𝄐	pause sign - play longer than usual
⊓	down bow →
V	up bow ←
4	4 bars' rest
1.	1st time bar - play first time
2.	2nd time bar - play on repeat
𝄋	Sign (segno) - repeat from here when you see 'D.S. al fine'
♩ = 120	metronome mark - 120 crotchets per minute

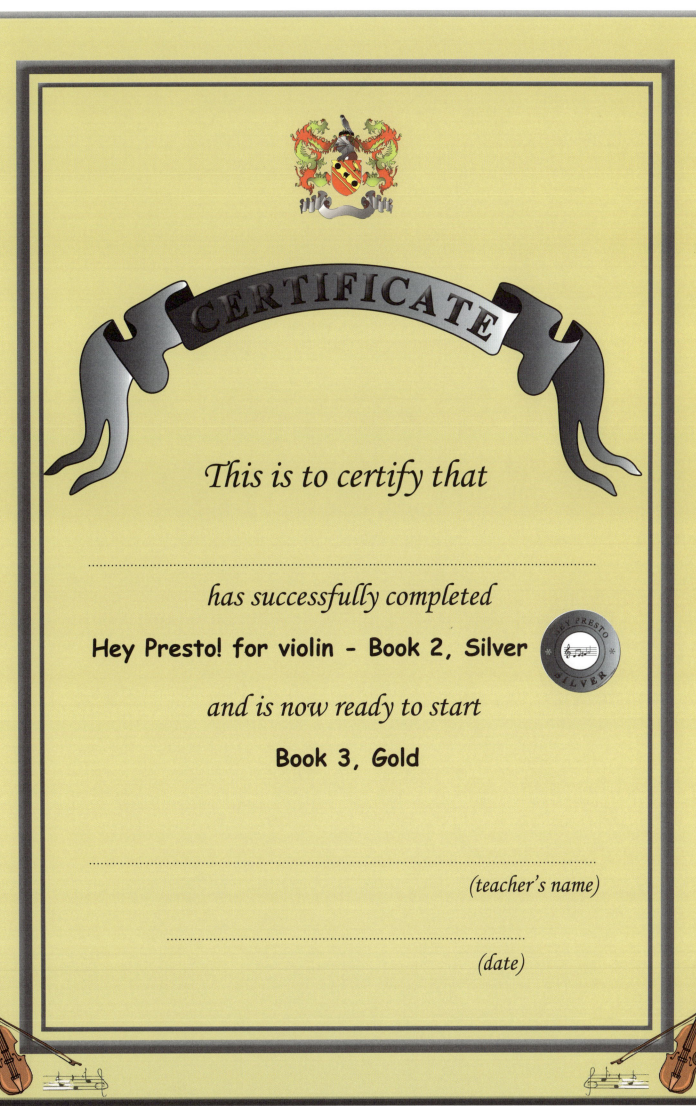